The Whole30 Instant Pot Cookbook

The Ultimate Whole30 Instant Pot Quick, Easy and Healthy Recipes for Your Multicooker and Instant Pot Pressure Cooker

Esther Rollins

© Copyright 2020 by Esther Rollins - All rights reserved.

This document is geared towards providing exact and reliable information in regard to the topic and issue covered. The publication is sold with the idea that the publisher is not required to render accounting, officially permitted, or otherwise, qualified services. If advice is necessary, legal or professional, a practiced individual in the profession should be ordered.

From a Declaration of Principles which was accepted and approved equally by a Committee of the American Bar Association and a Committee of Publishers and Associations. In no way is it legal to reproduce, duplicate, or transmit any part of this document in either electronic means or in printed format. Recording of this publication is strictly prohibited and any storage of this document is not allowed unless with written permission from the publisher. All rights reserved.

The information provided herein is stated to be truthful and consistent, in that any liability, in terms of inattention or otherwise, by any usage or abuse of any policies, processes, or directions contained within is the solitary and utter responsibility of the recipient reader. Under no circumstances will any legal responsibility or blame be held against the publisher for any reparation, damages, or monetary loss due to the information herein, either directly or indirectly.

Respective authors own all copyrights not held by the publisher.

Contents

Introduction 7

    The Rules of The Whole30 Diet Program............ 8

    Exception to The Rule 10

    What to Do for Thirty Days 12

Whole 30 Breakfast Recipes 15

    Eggs and Arugula..15

    Instant Pot Mini Frittatas................................... 16

    Easy Egg, Kale, And Beef Breakfast Muffins 17

    Instant Pot Egg "Bake" 18

    Whole30 Slow Cooked Breakfast Casserole 20

    Mexican Egg Casserole 21

    Kale and Red Pepper Frittata 23

    Breakfast Savory Pumpkin Porridge 24

    Breakfast Casserole with Chicken, Sweet Potatoes, And Kale 25

    Slow Cooker Sweet Potato Pesto Breakfast 27

    Steamed Egg Breakfast Muffins 28

    Instant Pot Green Eggs....................................... 29

Instant Pot Eggs in Cocotte 30

Spaghetti Squash Breakfast Casserole............... 32

Slow Cooked Breakfast Whole30 Meatzza 34

Scrambled Brussels Sprouts Breakfast Hash 35

Whole 30 Lunch Recipes 37

Yankee Pot Roast.. 37

Instant Pot Salsa Chicken...................................38

Whole30 Chicken Pho 40

Indian Lamb Curry... 42

Summer Italian Chicken..................................... 43

Slow Cooked Sweet Potato Curry Stew.............. 45

One Pot Coconut Chicken with Lemongrass 46

Instant Pot Mexican Beef 47

Korean Short Ribs 49

Whole 30 Chicken and Gravy 50

Braised Kale and Carrots....................................51

Tomato, Porcini, and Beef.................................. 52

Pineapple Chicken 54

Instant Pot Steamed Salmon.............................. 55

Chicken Adobo 56

Instant Pot Pork Carnitas 57

Whole 30 Dinner Recipes 59

Creamy Curried Broccoli Soup 59

Corned Beef and Cabbages 60

Instant Pot Steamed Artichokes 62

Instant Pot Bolognese Sauce 63

Asian Salmon with Vegetables 64

Instant Pot Ribs 66

Instant Pot Turkey Meatballs Soup 67

Ground Beef Goulash Soup 69

Asian Chicken with Lemongrass Soup 70

Instant Pot Kalua Pig 71

Simple Mocha Pot Roast 73

Jamaican Jerk Pork Roast 74

Beef Heart Chili 75

Easy Balsamic Pot Roast 77

Instant Pot Beef Stew 78

Italian Chicken Drumsticks with Garlic and Thyme 79

Whole 30 Dessert and Snacks Recipes 81

Steamed Almond Carrot Cake 81
Thai Coconut Pandan Custard......................... 82
Coconut Milk Yogurt 84
Cinnamon Bananas 85
Instant Pot Almond Cake 86
Slow Cooker Whole30 Berry Cobbler 87
Sweet Potato Puree.. 88
Baked Cinnamon Apples 89
Sautéed Apples and Pears 90
Cherry Crisps... 91
Instant Pot Applesauce..................................... 92
Strawberries with Coconut and Cashew Crumble 93
Slow-Cooked Peanut Butter Banana 94
Cocoa-Nut Apples... 95
Natural Fruit Preserves 96

Conclusion 99

INTRODUCTION

The kinds of foods that we eat greatly impact our health. Certain foods such as grains, dairy, sugar, and legumes can have negative impact in our health as they do not bring about obesity but other issues like skin allergies, digestive problems, chronic pain, and many others.

This is the reason why you have to strip your diet completely from foods that will be detrimental to your body. With the Whole30 Diet, you are encouraged to eliminate certain food groups that will encourage the cravings, disruption of blood sugar levels, damage the gut, and illicit inflammatory responses in the body for 30 days–no cheat days in between. With this particular diet, you allow your body to heal and recover from the effects of the food that you are traditionally consuming.

In a nutshell, this particular diet allows you to press the reset button not only with your health and habits but even your relationship with food. In turn, it affects you both physically and psychologically for the better. With this diet, you will change your life definitely!

The Rules of The Whole30 Diet Program

You are encouraged to eat healthy whole foods. Consume moderate amounts of meat, seafood, and eggs yet lots of vegetables, natural fats, herbs, spices, as well as some fruits. You know that the food that you are eating is compliant with the program when they are made from ingredients that you can recognize.

As such, there are some foods that you should avoid like the plague. These food, although considered healthy by many, can trigger inflammatory responses and other detrimental effects to the body. Below are the types of foods that you should avoid while following the Whole30 program.

- **No sugar of any kind:** Do not consume any kind of sugar – real or artificial – while following this program. This means that you should avoid, maple syrup, honey, agave,

coconut sugar, stevia, Equal, NutraSweet, Splenda, and xylitol to name a few.
- **Alcohol of any kind:** All types of alcohol, whether for drinking or cooking, are not allowed when following this program.
- **Grains:** Most grains are healthy but when you are following the Whole30 program, you should not consume grains of all forms. These include barley, corn, oats, bulgur, millet, sorghum, sprouted grains, amaranth, quinoa, and buckwheat.
- **Legumes:** Legumes are touted as healthy protein sources, but they contain lectins that drive the inflammatory responses in the body. This means that all kinds of beans and relatives of beans should not be consumed. These include black, red, white, navy, lima, fava, kidney, peas, lentils, chickpeas, and even peanuts. Legume-based products such as soy sauce, tempeh, tofu, and edamame are also not allowed with this diet.
- **Dairy:** Dairy from all animal sources are not allowed with the Whole30 diet program as they also trigger the inflammatory responses of the body. These include milk, sour cream,

butter, cheese, yogurt, and basically anything milk-based.

- **Sulfites, carrageenan, and MSG:** These food ingredients appear in many processed foods and beverages. These ingredients drive the inflammatory responses in the body. Thus, it is important to avoid the consumption of all types of processed and junk foods as they can compromise your health thus you will end up missing the point of following the Whole30 program. These include ice cream, muffins, pizzas, brownies, biscuits, cereals, canned meats, canned vegetables, and many others.

Exception to The Rule

While there are so many food categories that you are not allowed to consume while following the Whole30 diet program, there are certain foods that you are allowed to use so that you can consume to make your food flavorful. Below are the foods that are Whole30 compliant that you never thought they were.

- **Clarified butter or ghee:** Clarified butter or ghee is the only source of dairy that you are allowed to consume while following the Whole30 program as they have little impact to the body's inflammatory responses.
- **Fruit juice:** Fruit juice, as long as freshly squeezed and do not contain added or free sugar, as Whole30 compliant. So, if you are craving for fruit juice, make your own instead of buy the processed ones contained in cartons.
- **Some legumes:** Some legumes like sugar snap beans, green beans, and snow peas are Whole30 compliant. While they are technically legumes, they are consumed as pods more than as beans, so they don't really affect the inflammatory responses in the body.
- **Vinegar:** Vinegar of all forms such as white, red wine vinegar, balsamic, rice, and apple cider are allowed. However, the only exception is malt vinegar as it contains gluten.
- **Coconut aminos:** Use coconut aminos as an alternative to soy sauce. All brands of coconut aminos are Whole30 compliant as long as they do not come with added flavoring and ingredients.

- **Salt:** Salt is perhaps one of the most versatile seasoning that you can use to flavor your Whole30 compliant meals. Use only adequate amounts to flavor your food so as not to drive your blood pressure levels.

What to Do for Thirty Days

The only thing that you need to do while following the Whole30 program is to focus on making the right food choices. We are also not even recommending you weighing yourself daily nor counting the calories that you eat each day. The only way for this particular program to work is to stick by it for 30 days. This means that there are no cheats, slips, or even special occasions wherein you stop with the program to give in to your cravings. Remember that the Whole30 program is an elimination diet and re-introducing just a small amount of the foods that you are not allowed to consume can break the healing cycle of the body. You cannot say that you will eat your birthday cake tonight and resume with the Whole30 program the next day.

You might think it is hard but remember that fighting a severe illness is harder. Besides, this is just for thirty days. What you can do is to commit to the program wholeheartedly for 30 days. Anything else and you will never benefit from what the program has to offer. Short-selling yourself is cheating. In any case, it is only 30 days. If you don't feel happy, then by all means go back to your previous diet but we guarantee that you will be happy with the results.

WHOLE 30 BREAKFAST RECIPES

Eggs and Arugula
(Total Time: 8 Min|Serves: 6)

Ingredients
- 6 eggs, beaten
- ½ cup water
- Salt and pepper to taste
- A dash of dried oregano
- 1 cup arugula leaves, chopped

Instructions
1. Mix the egg and water in a bowl. Season with salt, pepper, and oregano to taste.
2. Grease the inside of the inner pot and place the arugula leaves.
3. Pour over the egg mixture.
4. Close the lid and seal the vent.
5. Press the Manual button and adjust the cooking time to 5 minutes.
6. Do natural pressure release.

Nutrition information:

Calories per serving:133; Carbohydrates: 1.8g; Protein: 9.2g; Fat: 9.6g; Sugar: 0.2g; Sodium: 104mg; Fiber: 1.1g

Instant Pot Mini Frittatas
(Total Time: 13 Min|Serves: 6)

Ingredients
- 5 eggs, beaten
- ½ cup almond milk, Whole30 compliant
- 1 teaspoon paprika
- Salt and pepper to taste
- 2 tablespoons chopped chives

Instructions
1. Place a trivet or a steam rack in the Instant Pot and pour a cup of water.
2. In a mixing bowl, combine all ingredients and mix until well-combined.
3. Pour into 6 individual molds and place gently on top of the steamer.
4. Close the lid and make sure that the vent is sealed.
5. Press the Steam button and adjust the cooking time to 8 minutes.

6. Do quick pressure release.

Nutrition information:
Calories per serving: 122; Carbohydrates: 3.7g; Protein:7.8 g; Fat: 8.4g; Sugar: 0.9g; Sodium: mg; 100Fiber: 0.4g

Easy Egg, Kale, And Beef Breakfast Muffins
(Total Time: 25 Min|Serves: 9)

Ingredients
- 9 large eggs, beaten
- 8 ounces ground beef
- 1 red pepper, seeded and chopped
- ½ cup frozen kale, chopped
- Salt and pepper to taste

Instructions
1. Place a trivet or steam rack on the Instant Pot. Pour a cup of water.
2. Combine all ingredients in a mixing bowl. Mix until well-combined.

3. Pour the contents into several greased molds.
4. Place the ramekins with the egg mixture on the trivet.
5. Close the lid and seal the vent.
6. Press the Steam button and adjust the cooking time to 20 minutes.
7. Do natural pressure release.

Nutrition information:
Calories per serving: 125; Carbohydrates: 1.9g; Protein: 9.4g; Fat: 8.6g; Sugar: 0g; Sodium: 102mg; Fiber: 0.5g

Instant Pot Egg "Bake"
(Total Time: 20 Min|Serves: 6)

Ingredients
- 6 eggs, beaten
- ¼ cup unsweetened almond milk, Whole30 compliant
- Salt and pepper to taste
- 1 cup cauliflower, grated
- 1 onion, minced

- ½ green sweet bell pepper, seeded and chopped
- ½ red sweet bell pepper, seeded and chopped

Instructions
1. In a mixing bowl, combine the eggs and almond. Season with salt and pepper until well combined.
2. Grease the inner pot with oil.
3. Place the cauliflower, onions, and bell peppers.
4. Pour over the mixture. Season with more salt and pepper to taste.
5. Close the lid and seal off the vent.
6. Press the Manual button and adjust the cooking time to 6 minutes.
7. Do natural pressure release.

Nutrition information:
Calories per serving: 151; Carbohydrates: 5.7g; Protein: 9.8g; Fat: 10.1g; Sugar: 1g; Sodium: 144mg; Fiber: 3.2g

Whole30 Slow Cooked Breakfast Casserole
(Total Time: 6 Hrs and 15 Min|Serves: 10)

Ingredients
- 3 tablespoons olive oil
- 1 cup lean ground beef, grass-fed
- ¼ onion, chopped
- 1 clove of garlic, crushed
- 8 ounces sliced mushrooms
- 1 large sweet potato, peeled and chopped
- 10 eggs, beaten
- Salt and pepper to taste
- Chopped green onions for garnish

Instructions
1. Press the Sauté button on the Instant Pot and heat the olive oil.
2. Stir in the ground beef and sauté for 3 minutes.
3. Add the onions and garlic. Continue stirring for another 2 minutes until fragrant and translucent.
4. Stir in the mushrooms and sweet potatoes and allow to cook for 2 minutes.

5. Pour the eggs and season with salt and pepper to taste.
6. Close the lid and don't seal the vent.
7. Press the Slow Cook button and cook for 6 hours.
8. Do natural pressure release.
9. Garnish with green onions.

Nutrition information:
Calories per serving: 222; Carbohydrates: 8.7g; Protein: 13.1; Fat: 14.9g; Sugar: 0g; Sodium: 119mg; Fiber: 3.2g

Mexican Egg Casserole
(Total Time: 25 Min|Serves: 8)

Ingredients
- 1-pound lean ground beef, grass-fed
- ½ onion, chopped
- 1 red bell pepper, seeded and chopped
- ½ teaspoon cumin powder
- ½ teaspoon oregano powder
- ½ teaspoon paprika

- Salt and pepper to taste
- 8 large eggs, beaten
- ½ cup water
- ½ cup chopped cilantro

Instructions
1. Press the Sauté button on the Instant Pot and sauté the beef and onions for 3 to 5 minutes or until the beef is lightly golden.
2. Add the bell pepper and season with cumin, oregano, paprika, salt, and pepper. Stir for 1 minute.
3. Pour in the eggs and water.
4. Close the lid and seal off the vent.
5. Press the Manual button and adjust the cooking time to 15 minutes.
6. Do natural pressure release.

Nutrition information:
Calories per serving: 184; Carbohydrates:2.4 g; Protein: 18.2g; Fat: 10.9g; Sugar: 1.1g; Sodium: 152mg; Fiber: 0.4g

Kale and Red Pepper Frittata
(Total Time: 5 Hrs and 5 Min|Serves: 8)

Ingredients
- 8 large eggs, beaten
- ½ cup coconut milk, Whole30 compliant
- 1 tablespoon coconut oil
- Salt and pepper to taste
- ½ cup red bell pepper, chopped
- 1 onion, chopped
- 2 cups chopped kale

Instructions
1. Mix the eggs, coconut milk, and oil in a bowl. Season with salt and pepper to taste.
2. Pour the red bell peppers, onion, and kale in the Instant Pot.
3. Pour the egg mixture.
4. Close the lid but do not seal the vent.
5. Press the Slow Cook button and adjust the cooking time to 5 hours.

Nutrition information:

Calories per serving: 115; Carbohydrates: 3.9g; Protein: 3.3g; Fat: 9.8g; Sugar: 0g; Sodium: 90mg; Fiber: 1.6g

Breakfast Savory Pumpkin Porridge
(Total Time: 30 Min|Serves: 6)

Ingredients
- ½ cup pumpkin, raw
- ½ cup coconut milk, freshly squeezed
- 1 cup water
- A dash of rosemary
- Salt and pepper to taste
- 1 egg, beaten

Instructions
1. Put all ingredients in the Instant Pot except for the egg.
2. Mix all the ingredients.
3. Close the lid and seal the vent.
4. Press the Soup button and adjust the cooking time to 15 minutes.
5. Do quick pressure release.

6. Once the lid is on, pour into the blender and add the egg. Pulse the mixture until smooth.
7. Place back into the Instant Pot and press the Sauté button.
8. Allow to simmer while stirring constantly for 5 minutes.

Nutrition information:

Calories per serving: 127; Carbohydrates: 3.4g; Protein: 5.1g; Fat: 11.2g; Sugar: 0g; Sodium: 47mg; Fiber: 1.5g

Breakfast Casserole with Chicken, Sweet Potatoes, And Kale

(Total Time: 20 Min|Serves: 6)

Ingredients
- 6 large eggs, beaten
- ¼ cup water
- 1 tablespoon olive oil
- 1 cup chicken breasts, chopped
- 1 onion, chopped

- 3 cloves of garlic, minced
- 1 large sweet potato, peeled and chopped
- 1 teaspoon cumin
- 1 teaspoon coriander
- Salt and pepper to taste
- 8 kale leaves, stems removed and torn into bite-sized pieces

Instructions

1. In a mixing bowl, combine the eggs and water. Set aside.
2. Press the Sauté button on the Instant Pot and heat the oil.
3. Stir in the chicken meat, onions, and garlic. Continue sautéing for 2 minutes before adding in the sweet potatoes.
4. Season with cumin, coriander, salt and pepper to taste.
5. Stir in the kale leaves and pour the egg mixture.
6. Close the lid and seal the vent.
7. Press the Manual button and adjust the cooking time to 10 minutes.
8. Do natural pressure release.

Nutrition information:

Calories per serving: 209; Carbohydrates: 11.7g; Protein: 14.9g; Fat: 11.6g; Sugar: 0.3g; Sodium: 60mg; Fiber: 3.6g

Slow Cooker Sweet Potato Pesto Breakfast
(Total Time: 6 Hrs and 10 Min|Serves: 4)

Ingredients
- 1 cup fresh basil
- 1 cup fresh kale
- 1/3 cup raw almonds
- 2 cloves of garlic, peeled
- 1 teaspoon salt
- ½ teaspoon ground black pepper
- 2 tablespoons extra virgin olive oil
- 1 large potato, peeled and sliced thinly
- 4 eggs, beaten

Instructions
1. Place the first 7 ingredients in a food processor. Pulse until smooth. This will be the pesto sauce. Set aside.

2. Place the potatoes in the Instant Pot and pour in the eggs. Season with salt and pepper.
3. Pour in the pesto sauce.
4. Close the lid and do not seal the vent.
5. Press the Slow Cook button and adjust the cooking time to 6 hours.

Nutrition information:

Calories per serving: 236; Carbohydrates: 18.6g; Protein: 11.4g; Fat: 12.8g; Sugar: 1.7g; Sodium: 201mg; Fiber: 2.4g

Steamed Egg Breakfast Muffins
(Total Time: 10 Min|Serves: 4)

Ingredients
- 8 eggs, beaten
- 1 cup diced broccoli florets
- 1 cup onion, minced
- 1 cup mushrooms, sliced
- Salt and pepper to taste

Instructions

1. Place a trivet or steam rack on the Instant Pot. Pour a cup of water.
2. Combine all ingredients in a mixing bowl. Mix until well-combined.
3. Pour the contents into several greased ramekins.
4. Place the ramekins with the egg mixture on the trivet.
5. Close the lid and seal the vent.
6. Press the Steam button and adjust the cooking time to 7 minutes.
7. Do natural pressure release.

Nutrition information:
Calories per serving: 278; Carbohydrates: 6.1g; Protein: 18.8g; Fat: 19.2g; Sugar: 0.9g; Sodium: 210mg; Fiber: 2.7g

Instant Pot Green Eggs
(Total Time: 8 Min|Serves: 6)

Ingredients
- 4 eggs, beaten
- 4 kale leaves, stems not removed

- 1 bunch of basil
- Salt and pepper to taste

Instructions
1. Place a trivet in the Instant Pot and pour a cup of water.
2. Place all ingredients in a food processor or blender.
3. Pulse until smooth.
4. Pour the green egg mixture into a heat-proof baking dish that will fit inside the Instant Pot.
5. Place the baking dish on top of the trivet.
6. Close the lid and seal the vent.
7. Press the Steam button and adjust the cooking time to 10 minutes.
8. Do quick pressure release.

Nutrition information:
Calories per serving: 142; Carbohydrates: 9.9g; Protein: 9.8g; Fat: 3.5g; Sugar: 0g; Sodium: 89mg; Fiber: 2.1g

Instant Pot Eggs in Cocotte
(Total Time: 13 Min|Serves: 3)

Ingredients
- 3 eggs, whole
- 3 tablespoons coconut milk
- 1 tablespoon chopped chives
- Salt and pepper to taste

Instructions
1. Place a trivet or a steam rack in the Instant Pot and pour a cup of water.
2. Get 3 ramekins and brush the insides with olive oil.
3. Crack an egg to each ramekin.
4. Place a tablespoon of coconut milk on top of each egg.
5. Sprinkle with chives and season with salt and pepper to taste.
6. Place the ramekins gently on the steam rack.
7. Close the lid and seal the vent.
8. Press the Steam button and adjust the cooking time to 10 minutes.
9. Do quick pressure release.

Nutrition information:
Calories per serving: 170; Carbohydrates: 3.3g; Protein: 9.6g; Fat: 13.3; Sugar: 0g; Sodium: 124mg; Fiber: 0g

Spaghetti Squash Breakfast Casserole
(Total Time: 35 Min | Serves: 4)

Ingredients
- 1 medium-sized spaghetti squash, halved and seeded
- Salt and pepper to taste
- 2 tablespoons olive oil
- 1 cup lean ground beef, grass-fed
- 1 cup onion, diced
- 2 cloves of garlic, minced
- ½ teaspoon dried Italian seasoning
- ½ cup organic tomatoes, diced
- 4 large eggs, whole
- Chopped parsley for garnish

Instructions
1. Place a trivet or a steam rack in the Instant Pot and pour a cup of water. Season the spaghetti squash with salt and pepper to taste and place on the steam rack.
2. Close the lid and seal the vent. Press the Steam button and adjust the cooking time to 10 minutes. Do quick pressure release.
3. Take the squash out and shred the "meat" using a fork. Set aside.

4. Clean the Instant Pot and remove the water and trivet.
5. Press the Sauté button and heat the oil. Stir in the beef, onions, and garlic. Continue stirring for about 3 minutes until the meat has turned lightly golden.
6. Add the Italian seasonings and tomatoes. Stir in the shredded spaghetti squash. Season with more salt and pepper to taste.
7. Gently crack the four eggs on top of the vegetable mixture.
8. Close the lid and seal the vent.
9. Press the Manual button and adjust the cooking time to 10 minutes.
10. Do natural pressure release.
11. Garnish with chopped parsley.

Nutrition information:
Calories per serving: 333; Carbohydrates: 17g; Protein: 14g; Fat: 23g; Sugar:0g; Sodium: 417mg; Fiber: 3.7g

Slow Cooked Breakfast Whole30 Meatzza

(Total Time: 8 Hrs and 10 Min|Serves: 4)

Ingredients

- 7 eggs, beaten
- 1 cup water
- Salt and pepper to taste
- 1-pound lean ground beef
- 1 yellow onion, diced
- 1 clove of garlic, minced
- ½ sweet potato, peeled and diced

Instructions

1. In a mixing bowl, mix the eggs and water until well combined. Season with salt and pepper to taste.
2. Press the Sauté button on the Instant Pot and stir in the beef for 2 minutes.
3. Stir in the onion and garlic until fragrant.
4. Add the sweet potatoes and continue stirring for another 3 more minutes.
5. Pour in the egg mixture.
6. Close the lid and do not seal the vent.
7. Press the Slow Cook button and adjust the cooking time to 8 hours.

Nutrition information:

Calories per serving: 479; Carbohydrates: 3.8g; Protein: 46.7g; Fat: 29.5g; Sugar: 0.2g; Sodium: 271mg; Fiber: 1.4g

Scrambled Brussels Sprouts Breakfast Hash

(Total Time: 30 Min | Serves: 6)

Ingredients

- 1-pound lean ground beef
- 1 onion, diced
- 2 cloves of garlic, minced
- 1 sweet potato, peeled and cut into cubes
- 12 Brussels sprouts, stems removed and halved
- Salt and pepper to taste
- 4 large eggs, beaten

Instructions

1. Press the Sauté button on the Instant Pot and stir in the beef, onion, and garlic.

2. Continue cooking until the meat has turned lightly golden and the spices fragrant.
3. Stir in the potatoes and Brussels sprouts. Season with salt and pepper to taste.
4. Add ½ cup of water.
5. Close the lid and seal the vent.
6. Press the Manual button and adjust the cooking time to 15 minutes.
7. Do quick pressure release to open the lid.
8. Once the lid is open, press the Sauté button and continue simmering until the sauce has reduced.
9. Pour in the eggs and continue stirring until the egg is scrambled.
10. Season with more salt and pepper if needed.

Nutrition information:
Calories per serving: 245; Carbohydrates: 10.9g; Protein: 23.9g; Fat: 11.6g; Sugar: 1.4g; Sodium: 132mg; Fiber: 4.2g

WHOLE 30 LUNCH RECIPES

Yankee Pot Roast
(Total Time: 1 Hr and 20 Min|Serves: 6)

Ingredients
- 1-pound beef chuck roast, bone removed
- Salt and pepper to taste
- 2 tablespoons coconut oil
- 1 celery stalk, chopped
- 2 cloves of garlic, minced
- 1 onion, quartered
- 1 carrot, chopped
- 1 tablespoon organic tomato paste
- ½ ounce porcini mushrooms
- 2 sprigs fresh thyme
- 1 cup water
- ½ cup chopped Italian parsley

Instructions
1. Season the meat with salt and pepper to taste.
2. Press the Sauté button on the Instant Pot and heat the oil. Stir in the celery, garlic, and onions until fragrant
3. Add the meat and sear on all sides.

4. Toss in the carrots, tomato paste, mushrooms, and thyme. Pour water.
5. Scrape the bottom of the pot to remove the browning.
6. Close the lid and seal the vent.
7. Press the Manual button and adjust the cooking time to 60 minutes.
8. Do natural pressure release.
9. Garnish with Italian parsley.

Nutrition information:

Calories per serving: 204; Carbohydrates: 6.2g; Protein: 21.1g; Fat: 11.1g; Sugar: 1.3g; Sodium: 86mg; Fiber: 2.4g

Instant Pot Salsa Chicken
(Total Time: 45 Min|Serves: 6)

Ingredients
- 2 pounds boneless chicken breasts
- 1 ½ chili powder
- 1 teaspoon cumin powder
- 1 teaspoon paprika

- 1 teaspoon dried oregano
- 1 cup chopped tomatoes
- Salt and pepper to taste
- 1 cup chopped cilantro
- ½ of avocado, sliced

Instructions
1. Place the chicken in the Instant Pot.
2. Add the chili powder, cumin, paprika, oregano, and tomatoes. Season with salt and pepper to taste.
3. Adjust the water to add more moisture.
4. Close the lid and seal the vent.
5. Press the Poultry button and adjust the cooking time to 30 minutes.
6. Do natural pressure release.
7. Serve and garnish with cilantro and avocado slices.

Nutrition information:
Calories per serving: 219; Carbohydrates: 3.6g; Protein: 34.9g; Fat: 6.6g; Sugar: 1.2g; Sodium: 73mg; Fiber: 1.8g

Whole30 Chicken Pho
(Total Time: 1 Hr and 5 Min|Serves: 4)

Ingredients
- 1 tablespoon coriander seeds
- 3 whole cloves
- 2-inch ginger, crushed
- 1 onion, halved
- 7 cups water
- 1-pound whole chicken
- 1 small apple, cored and peeled
- ¾ cup cilantro sprigs
- Salt and pepper to taste
- 4 zucchinis, spiralized into noodles
- ½ red onion, sliced thinly
- 2 stalks of green onions, chopped
- 4 lime wedges

Instructions
1. In the Instant Pot, place all the coriander seeds, cloves, ginger, and onion.

2. Press the Sauté button and allow to toast for 2 minutes.

3. Pour in the water, chicken, apple, and cilantro. Season with salt and pepper to taste.

4. Close the lid and seal the vent.
5. Press the Poultry button and adjust the cooking time to 50 minutes.
6. Do quick pressure release.
7. Take the chicken out and shred the meat and discard the bones. Set the meat aside.
8. Strain the liquid and discard the spices. This will serve as the broth.
9. On four bowls, arrange the zucchini noodles and red onions.
10. Add chicken meat and pour in broth.
11. Garnish with green onions and lime wedges.

Nutrition information:
Calories per serving: 284; Carbohydrates: 36g; Protein: 19.6g; Fat: 8.6g; Sugar: 5g; Sodium: 425mg; Fiber: 10.4g

Indian Lamb Curry
(Total Time: 1 Hr and 30 Min|Serves: 6)

Ingredients
- 1 tablespoon coconut oil
- 2 ½ pounds lamb spare ribs
- Salt and pepper to taste
- 1 tablespoon curry powder
- 1 onion, chopped
- 5 cloves garlic, minced
- ½ pound ripe tomatoes, chopped
- Juice of 1 lemon, freshly squeezed
- 2 cups water
- 1 ¼ cup chopped cilantro

Instructions
1. Press the Sauté button on the Instant Pot and heat the oil.
2. Stir in the lamb spare ribs and season with salt, pepper, and curry powder.
3. Add the onions and garlic.
4. Stir for 3 minutes or until fragrant.
5. Pour in the tomatoes and lemon juice.
6. Add water and season with more salt and pepper as needed.
7. Close the lid and seal the vent.

8. Press the Meat/Stew button and adjust the cooking time to 60 minutes.
9. Do natural pressure release.
10. Garnish with chopped cilantro.

Nutrition information:
Calories per serving: 366; Carbohydrates: 5.9g; Protein: 38.8g; Fat: 20.1g; Sugar: 2.4g; Sodium: 143mg; Fiber: 1.9g

Summer Italian Chicken
(Total Time: 55 Min|Serves: 8)

Ingredients
- 8 boneless chicken thighs
- Salt and pepper to taste
- 1 tablespoon olive oil
- 1 onion, chopped
- 3 cloves of garlic, minced
- 2 medium carrots, chopped
- ½ pound cremini mushrooms, sliced
- 2 cups cherry tomatoes, chopped
- 1 cup water

- 1 cup basil leaves
- 1 cup Italian parsley, chopped

Instructions
1. Season the chicken thighs with salt and pepper to taste.
2. Press the Sauté button on the Instant Pot and heat the oil. Stir in the seasoned chicken, onion, and garlic.
3. Stir for 3 minutes until fragrant and the chicken has turned lightly golden.
4. Add the carrots, mushrooms, cherry tomatoes and water. Season with more salt and pepper if necessary.
5. Close the lid and seal the vent.
6. Press the Poultry button and adjust the cooking time to 30 minutes.
7. Do quick pressure release.
8. Once the lid is open, press the Sauté button and add the basil and parsley. Simmer for 3 minutes.

Nutrition information:
Calories per serving: 563; Carbohydrates: 44.7g; Protein: 28.6g; Fat: 31.9g; Sugar: 1.5g; Sodium: 901mg; Fiber: 4.3g

Slow Cooked Sweet Potato Curry Stew
(Total Time: 30 Min | Serves: 3)

Ingredients
- 1 tablespoon olive oil
- 1 onion, diced
- 2-inch piece fresh ginger, sliced
- 2 cloves of garlic, minced
- 2 sweet potatoes, peeled and diced
- 1 zucchini, diced
- 1 cup diced tomatoes
- 2 teaspoons curry powder
- 1 teaspoon turmeric powder
- Salt and pepper to taste
- 2 cups coconut milk, freshly squeezed
- ½ cup water

Instructions
1. Press the Sauté button on the Instant Pot and heat the oil.
2. Sauté the onion, ginger, and garlic for 1 minute.
3. Add the sweet potatoes, zucchini, tomatoes, curry powder and turmeric powder.
4. Stir for another minute and season with salt and pepper to taste.

5. Add the coconut milk and water.
6. Close the lid and seal the vent.
7. Press the Manual button and adjust the cooking time to 10 minutes.
8. Do quick pressure release.
9. Garnish with cilantro and lime wedges if desired.

Nutrition information:

Calories per serving: 450; Carbohydrates: 18.1g; Protein: 5.3g; Fat: 43.1g; Sugar: 4g; Sodium: 31mg; Fiber: 9.8g

One Pot Coconut Chicken with Lemongrass
(Total Time: 55 Min|Serves: 10)

Ingredients
- 1 stalk lemongrass, cut into an inch thick
- 4 cloves of garlic, peeled and crushed
- 1 thumb-size ginger, crushed
- 1 teaspoon Chinese five spice powder

- 1 cup coconut milk, freshly squeezed
- 10 chicken drumsticks, skin removed
- Juice of 1 lime, freshly squeezed

Instructions
1. Place all ingredients in the Instant Pot.
2. Give a good stir.
3. Close the lid and seal the vent.
4. Press the Manual button and adjust the cooking time to 25 minutes.
5. Do natural pressure release.

Nutrition information:

Calories per serving: 268; Carbohydrates: 2.3g; Protein: 24.2g; Fat: 17.7g; Sugar: 0.8g; Sodium: 142mg; Fiber:0.9g

Instant Pot Mexican Beef
(Total Time: 1 Hr and 25 Min|Serves: 8)

Ingredients
- 1 ½ tablespoon coconut oil
- 2 ½ pound beef short ribs, bones removed and cut into chunks

- Salt and pepper to taste
- 1 tablespoon chili powder
- 1 onion, sliced
- 6 cloves of garlic, crushed
- ½ cup chopped tomatoes
- 1 cup water
- 2 radishes, roughly chopped

Instructions

1. Press the Sauté button on the Instant Pot and heat the oil.
2. Stir in the beef short ribs and season with salt, pepper, and chili powder.
3. Add the onions and garlic.
4. Stir for 3 minutes.
5. Add the tomatoes, water, and radishes.
6. Close the lid and seal the vent.
7. Press the Meat/Stew button and adjust the cooking time to 60 minutes.
8. Do natural pressure release.

Nutrition information:

Calories per serving: 276; Carbohydrates: 5.7g; Protein: 29.5g; Fat: 15.6g; Sugar: 1.6g; Sodium: 180mg; Fiber: 2.5g

Korean Short Ribs

(Total Time: 1 Hr and 25 Min|Serves: 12)

Ingredients
- 5 pounds short ribs, bone in
- Salt and pepper to taste
- ½ cup coconut aminos
- 1 tablespoon lemon juice, freshly squeezed
- 1 peeled medium pear, cored and chopped
- 6 cloves of garlic, minced
- 1 fresh ginger, sliced thinly
- 1 cup water
- 3 scallions, chopped
- 2 tablespoons sesame seeds, toasted

Instructions
1. Place short ribs in the Instant Pot and season with salt and pepper to taste.
2. Press the Sauté button and stir for 3 minutes.
3. Add the coconut aminos, lemon juice, pear, garlic, and ginger. Stir for another minute. Add water.
4. Close the lid and seal off the vent.
5. Press the Meat/Stew button and adjust the cooking time to 60 minutes.
6. Do natural pressure release.

7. Once the lid is open, give another stir and garnish with scallions and sesame seeds.

Nutrition information:

Calories per serving: 743; Carbohydrates:21.1g; Protein: 81.9g; Fat: 27.9g; Sugar: 6.6g; Sodium: 126mg; Fiber: 5.2g

Whole 30 Chicken and Gravy
(Total Time: 50 Min|Serves: 6)

Ingredients
- 1 whole chicken, cut into parts
- Salt and pepper to taste
- 2 onions, chopped
- 6 cloves of garlic, minced
- 2 teaspoons organic tomato paste
- ½ cup water

Instructions
1. Place all ingredients in the Instant Pot.
2. Give a good stir.
3. Close the lid and seal the vent.
4. Press the Poultry button and adjust the cooking time to 30 minutes.

5. Do natural pressure release.

Nutrition information:
Calories per serving: 353; Carbohydrates: 5.3g; Protein: 29.3g; Fat: 23.2g; Sugar: 0.5g; Sodium: 111mg; Fiber: 2.1g

Braised Kale and Carrots
(Total Time: 20 Min|Serves: 2)

Ingredients
- 1 tablespoon coconut oil
- 1 onion, sliced thinly
- 5 cloves of garlic, minced
- 3 medium carrots, sliced thinly
- 10 ounces of kale, chopped
- ½ cup water
- Salt and pepper to taste
- A dash of red pepper flakes

Instructions
1. Press the Sauté button on the Instant Pot and heat the oil
2. Toss in the onions and garlic until fragrant.

3. Toss in the carrots and stir for 30 seconds. Add the kale and water. Season with salt and pepper to taste.
4. Close the lid and seal the vent.
5. Press the Manual button and adjust the cooking time to 5 minutes.
6. Do quick pressure release.
7. Once cooked, garnish with red pepper flakes.

Nutrition information:

Calories per serving: 161; Carbohydrates: 19.9g; Protein: 7.5g; Fat: 8.2g; Sugar: 6.1g; Sodium: 63mg; Fiber: 5.9g

Tomato, Porcini, and Beef
(Total Time: 1 Hr and 55 Min|Serves: 12)

Ingredients
- 1 tablespoon coconut oil
- 5 pounds beef short ribs, cut into cubes
- Salt and pepper to taste
- 1 onion, chopped
- 2 cloves of garlic, minced

- 2 celery stalks, chopped
- 2 cups chopped tomatoes
- ½ ounce porcini mushrooms, sliced
- 1 cup boiling water

Instructions

1. Press the Sauté button on the Instant Pot and heat the oil.
2. Stir in the beef and season with salt and pepper to taste.
3. Add the onions, garlic, and tomatoes. Continue stirring for another 2 minutes.
4. Stir in the rest of the ingredients.
5. Close the lid and seal the vent.
6. Press the Meat/Stew button and adjust the cooking time to 1 hour and 30 minutes.
7. Do natural pressure release.

Nutrition information:

Calories per serving: 342; Carbohydrates: 5.6g; Protein: 39.1g; Fat: 18.5g; Sugar: 1g; Sodium: 190mg; Fiber: 1.3g

Pineapple Chicken
(Total Time: 60 Min|Serves: 9)

Ingredients
- 3 pounds chicken breasts
- Salt and pepper to taste
- ½ pineapple fruit, peeled and cut into small sliced
- 4 cloves of garlic, minced
- 1 cup onion, diced
- 2 tablespoons coconut aminos
- 1-inch ginger, sliced
- 1 cup water

Instructions
1. Place all ingredients in the Instant Pot.
2. Mix all ingredients until well-combined.
3. Close the lid and seal the vent.
4. Press the Poultry button and adjust the cooking time to 35 minutes.
5. Do natural pressure release.

Nutrition information:
Calories per serving: 320; Carbohydrates: 15.7g; Protein:32.5 g; Fat: 14.4g; Sugar: 6.8g; Sodium: 101mg; Fiber: 4.6g

Instant Pot Steamed Salmon
(Total Time: 25 Min|Serves: 4)

Ingredients
- 4 salmon fillets, skin removed
- A pinch of dried sage or rosemary
- 4 tablespoons lemon juice, freshly squeezed
- Salt and pepper to taste

Instructions
1. Place a trivet or a steam rack in the Instant Pot and pour a cup of water.
2. Place all ingredients in a bowl and mix until well combined.
3. Place the fish on the trivet.
4. Close the lid and seal the vent.
5. Press the Steam button and adjust the cooking time to 15 minutes.
6. Do quick pressure release.

Nutrition information:
Calories per serving: 398; Carbohydrates: 2.1g; Protein: 65.4g; Fat: 14.5g; Sugar: 0.2g; Sodium: 954mg; Fiber: 0.9g

Chicken Adobo
(Total Time: 40 Min|Serves: 6)

Ingredients
- 2 pounds chicken meat
- ¼ cup coconut aminos
- ¼ cup lemon juice, freshly squeezed
- 1 bay leaf
- Salt and pepper to taste

Instructions
1. Place all ingredients in the Instant Pot.
2. Give a good stir.
3. Close the lid and seal the vent.
4. Press the Manual button and adjust the cooking time to 30 minutes.
5. Do natural pressure release.

Nutrition information:
Calories per serving: 245; Carbohydrates: 1.8g; Protein: 30.1g; Fat: 12.3g; Sugar: 0.3g; Sodium: 114mg; Fiber: 0.9g

Instant Pot Pork Carnitas

(Total Time: 1 Hr and 50 Min|Serves: 9)

Ingredients
- 3 pounds pork shoulder roast, bone in
- 2 teaspoons ground cumin
- 1 teaspoon crushed red pepper flakes
- Teaspoon dried oregano leaves
- 1 medium orange fruit, peeled and segmented
- 6 cloves of garlic, minced
- 1 onion, peeled and quartered
- 1 bay leaf
- 1 sprig cilantro, chopped

Instructions
1. Place all ingredients in the Instant Pot.
2. Give a good stir.
3. Close the lid and seal the vent.
4. Press the Manual button and adjust the cooking time to 1 hour and 30 minutes.
5. Do natural pressure release.
6. Take the meat out and shred using a fork. Discard the bone.
7. Serve on top of lettuce leaves.

Nutrition information:

Calories per serving: 370; Carbohydrates: 4.5g; Protein: 37.2g; Fat: 21.7g; Sugar: 0.9g; Sodium: 135mg; Fiber: 2.3g

WHOLE 30 DINNER RECIPES

Creamy Curried Broccoli Soup
(Total Time: 1 Hr and 25 Min|Serves: 5)

Ingredients
- 5 cups water
- 1-pound chicken bones
- 2 tablespoons coconut oil
- 2 shallots, chopped
- 1 tablespoon Indian curry powder
- 1 ½ pounds broccoli, chopped into florets
- ¼ cup, apple, peeled and diced
- 1 cup coconut milk, freshly squeezed

Instructions
1. Place the water and chicken bones in the Instant Pot.
2. Close the lid and seal the vent.
3. Press the Manual button and adjust the cooking time to 50 minutes.
4. Do natural pressure release.
5. Strain the broth and discard the bones. Set the broth aside.

6. Press the Sauté button on the Instant Pot and heat the coconut oil.
7. Sauté the onions and stir for 1 minute. Stir in the curry powder and toast for 30 seconds.
8. Add the broccoli and apple. Pour in the broth and coconut milk.
9. Close the lid and seal the vent.
10. Press the Soup button and adjust the cooking time to 5 minutes.
11. Do natural pressure release.

Nutrition information:
Calories per serving: 298; Carbohydrates: 8.6g; Protein: 24.5g; Fat:20.9 g; Sugar: 2.6g; Sodium:126mg; Fiber: 5.7g

Corned Beef and Cabbages
(Total Time: 1 Hr and 55 Min|Serves: 12)

Ingredients
- 4 pounds corned beef brisket, bones removed and cut into chunks
- 6 cups water

- Salt and pepper to taste
- 4 cloves of garlic, minced
- 2 teaspoon dried mustard powder
- 2 onions, chopped
- 4 carrots, chopped
- 4 celery stalks, chopped
- 1 head cabbage, cut into wedges

Instructions
1. Place all ingredients in the Instant Pot except for the cabbage.
2. Give a good stir and close the lid.
3. Seal the vent.
4. Press the Manual button and adjust the cooking time to 1 hour and 30 minutes.
5. Do quick pressure release.
6. Once the lid is open, press the Sauté button and Add the cabbage.
7. Allow to simmer for 5 minutes.

Nutrition information:
Calories per serving: 334; Carbohydrates: 8.1g; Protein: 23.7g; Fat: 22.8g; Sugar: 0g; Sodium: 1,882mg; Fiber: 4.6g

Instant Pot Steamed Artichokes
(Total Time: 30 Min|Serves: 2)

Ingredients
- 1 whole artichokes
- 1 lemon wedge
- Salt and pepper to taste

Instructions
1. Place a trivet or a steam rack in the Instant Pot and pour a cup of water.
2. Season the artichokes with a lemon wedge, salt, and pepper.
3. Place on the steamer.
4. Close the lid and seal the vent.
5. Press the Steam button and adjust the cooking time to 25 minutes.
6. Do natural pressure release.

Nutrition information:
Calories per serving: 52; Carbohydrates: 12.3g; Protein: 3.1g; Fat: 0.2g; Sugar: 0g; Sodium: 41mg; Fiber: 8.5g

Instant Pot Bolognese Sauce
(Total Time: 65 Min|Serves: 6)

Ingredients
- 2 tablespoons olive oil
- 1 large onion, chopped
- 4 cloves of garlic, minced
- 2 pounds lean ground beef
- 1 teaspoon paprika powder
- ½ teaspoon cinnamon powder
- 2 tablespoons coconut aminos
- Salt and pepper to taste
- 1 carrots, diced small
- 2 celery sticks, diced small
- Salt and pepper to taste
- 2 bay leaves
- 4 cups chopped tomatoes
- 2 cups water

Instructions
1. Press the Sauté button on the Instant Pot and heat the oil.
2. Stir in the onion and garlic until fragrant.
3. Add the ground beef and season with paprika, cinnamon, and coconut aminos. Season with more salt and pepper to taste if desired.

4. Continue stirring for 3 minutes.
5. Add the rest of the ingredients.
6. Close the lid and seal the vent.
7. Press the Manual button and adjust the cooking time to 40 minutes.
8. Do natural pressure release.

Nutrition information:
Calories per serving: 407; Carbohydrates: 9.8g; Protein: 42.1g; Fat: 21.6g; Sugar: 2.5g; Sodium: 117mg; Fiber: 5.1g

Asian Salmon with Vegetables
(Total Time: 30 Min|Serves: 2)

Ingredients
- 2 salmon fillets
- 1 clove of garlic, minced
- 2 teaspoons grated ginger
- 2 tablespoons coconut aminos
- Salt and pepper to taste
- 1 large carrot, peeled and julienned
- 1 cup broccoli, cut into florets

- 1 tablespoon sesame oil
- ½ tablespoons sesame seeds, toasted

Instructions

1. Place a trivet or steam rack in the Instant Pot. Pour a cup of water.
2. In a bowl, season the salmon fillets with garlic, ginger, coconut aminos, salt, and pepper.
3. Place the fillet on the steam rack. Lay the carrots and broccoli florets beside the fillets.
4. Close the lid and seal the vent.
5. Press the Steam button and adjust the cooking time to 15 minutes.
6. Do quick pressure release.
7. Place the fillets and vegetables on a plate and drizzle with sesame oil.
8. Garnish with toasted sesame seeds on top.

Nutrition information:

Calories per serving: 281; Carbohydrates: 7.9g; Protein: 25.6g; Fat: 16.4g; Sugar: 2.1g; Sodium: 541mg; Fiber: 3.3g

Instant Pot Ribs
(Total Time: 1 Hr and 55 Min|Serves: 14)

Ingredients
- 5 pounds pork ribs
- Salt and pepper to taste
- 3 cloves of garlic, minced
- 1 onion, minced
- 1 teaspoon paprika
- ½ teaspoon allspice
- ½ coriander powder
- 2 tablespoons lemon juice, freshly squeezed
- 1 peeled apple, cored and chopped

Instructions
1. Place all ingredients in the Instant Pot except for the cabbage.
2. Give a good stir and close the lid. Seal the vent.
3. Press the Manual button and adjust the cooking time to 1 hour and 30 minutes.
4. Do quick pressure release.

Nutrition information:

Calories per serving: 240; Carbohydrates: 3.3g; Protein: 33.8g; Fat: 9.2g; Sugar: 0.6g; Sodium: 109mg; Fiber: 1.9g

Instant Pot Turkey Meatballs Soup
(Total Time: 3 Hrs and 5 Min|Serves: 6)

Ingredients
- 1 ½ pounds ground turkey meat
- 2 tablespoons fresh cilantro
- ½ long red chili, chopped
- ½ teaspoon white pepper
- ½ teaspoon salt
- 2 teaspoons sesame oil
- 2 eggs, beaten
- 1 tablespoon coconut oil
- 2 cloves of garlic, grated
- 1 teaspoon grated ginger
- 4 cups water
- 1 teaspoon fish sauce
- 2 tablespoons black and white sesame seeds, toasted

Instructions

1. Place the first seven ingredients in a mixing bowl. Mix until well-combined. Form small meatballs using the palm of your hands. Place in the fridge and allow to set for 2 hours.
2. Press the Sauté button on the Instant Pot and heat the oil.
3. Add the meatballs and allow to sear the surface for 3 minutes.
4. Add the garlic, ginger, and water. Season with fish sauce, salt, and pepper.
5. Close the lid and seal the vent.
6. Press the Manual button and adjust the cooking time to 30 minutes.
7. Do natural pressure release.
8. Garnish with sesame seeds on top.

Nutrition information:

Calories per serving: 262; Carbohydrates: 1.6g; Protein: 25.8g; Fat: 16.9g; Sugar: 0.2g; Sodium: 377mg; Fiber: 0.5g

Ground Beef Goulash Soup
(Total Time: 55 Min|Serves: 6)

Ingredients
- 2 teaspoons olive oil
- 1 ½ pound lean ground beef
- 1 onion, sliced
- 3 cloves of garlic, minced
- 2 tablespoons paprika
- 4 cups water
- 1 zucchini, chopped
- 1 carrot, chopped
- 2 cups tomatoes, diced
- Salt and pepper to taste

Instructions
1. Press the Sauté button on the Instant Pot and heat oil.
2. Stir in the beef, onion, and garlic. Continue stirring for 3 minutes.
3. Add the rest of the ingredients.
4. Season with salt and pepper to taste.
5. Close the lid and seal the lid.
6. Press the Manual button and adjust the cooking time to 30 minutes.

7. Do quick pressure release.

Nutrition information:
Calories per serving: 282; Carbohydrates: 5.5g; Protein: 31.4g; Fat: 14.5g; Sugar: 1.9g; Sodium: 84mg; Fiber: 2.6g

Asian Chicken with Lemongrass Soup
(Total Time: 35 Min|Serves: 5)

Ingredients
- 1-pound chicken breasts
- 5 cups water
- 1 cup chopped tomatoes
- 1-inch ginger, sliced
- 1 onion, quartered
- 1 stalk lemongrass
- Salt and pepper to taste
- 1 cup basil leaves

Instructions
1. Place all ingredients except for the basil in the Instant Pot.

2. Give a good stir.
3. Close the lid and seal the vent.
4. Press the Poultry button and adjust the cooking time to 20 minutes.
5. Do quick pressure release.
6. Once the lid is open, press the Sauté button and stir in the basil leaves.
7. Allow to simmer for 3 minutes.

Nutrition information:

Calories per serving: 174; Carbohydrates: 4.2g; Protein: 19.6g; Fat:8.5 g; Sugar: 0.9g; Sodium: 65mg; Fiber: 2.9g

Instant Pot Kalua Pig
(Total Time: 2 Hrs and 20 Min|Serves: 14)

Ingredients
- 5 pounds pork shoulder roast, bone in
- 5 cloves of garlic, minced
- Salt and pepper to taste
- 1 cup water
- 1 cabbage, cut into wedges

Instructions
1. Place all ingredients except for the cabbages in the Instant Pot.
2. Close the lid and seal the vent.
3. Press the Manual button and adjust the cooking time to 2 hours.
4. Do quick pressure release.
5. Once the lid is open, take the meat out and shred with a fork.
6. Place the meat back into the Instant Pot and press the Sauté button.
7. Stir in the cabbages and simmer for another 5 minutes.

Nutrition information:
Calories per serving: 404; Carbohydrates: 6.6g; Protein: 40.5g; Fat: 23.1g; Sugar: 1.2g; Sodium: 327mg; Fiber: 3.4g

Simple Mocha Pot Roast
(Total Time: 3 Hrs and 45 Min|Serves: 8)

Ingredients
- 2 tablespoons ground coffee
- 2 tablespoons smoke paprika
- 1 tablespoon cocoa powder
- 1 teaspoon chili powder
- Salt and pepper to taste
- 2 pounds beef chuck roast
- 3 tablespoons olive oil
- 1 cup water
- 1 onion, chopped
- 6 dried figs, chopped
- 3 tablespoons lemon juice

Instructions
1. In a bowl, combine the ground coffee, paprika, cocoa powder, chili powder, salt pepper, and beef chuck roast. Coat the beef with the spices and marinate in the fridge for at least 3 hours.
2. Press the Sauté button on the Instant Pot and heat the oil.
3. Sear the beef chuck roast on all sides until lightly brown.

4. Add the rest of the ingredients. Season with more salt and pepper if desired.
5. Close the lid and seal the vent.
6. Press the Manual button and adjust the cooking time to 1 hour and 30 minutes.
7. Do natural pressure release.

Nutrition information:
Calories per serving: 284; Carbohydrates: 7.7g; Protein: 31.2g; Fat:15.1 g; Sugar: 1.9g; Sodium: 104mg; Fiber: 4.5g

Jamaican Jerk Pork Roast
(Total Time: 1 Hr and 35 Min|Serves: 10)

Ingredients
- 4 pounds pork shoulder
- ¼ cup sugar-free Jamaican spice blend, Whole 30 compliant
- 1 cup water

Instructions
1. Place all ingredients in the Instant Pot except for the cabbage.
2. Give a good stir and close the lid.

3. Seal the vent.
4. Press the Manual button and adjust the cooking time to 1 hour and 30 minutes.
5. Do quick pressure release.

Nutrition information:
Calories per serving: 485; Carbohydrates: 0.3g; Protein: 45.5g; Fat: 32.1g; Sugar: 0g; Sodium: 108mg; Fiber: 0g

Beef Heart Chili
(Total Time: 1 Hr and 20 Min|Serves: 4)

Ingredients
- 1 tablespoon olive oil
- 4 cloves of garlic, minced
- 1 jalapeno, chopped
- 1 onion, chopped
- 1-pound ground beef
- ½ pound beef heart, trimmed and cut into strips
- 3 tablespoons Mexican chili powder
- 1 tablespoon ground cumin

- 2 teaspoons dried oregano
- Salt and pepper to taste
- 2 cups chopped tomatoes
- 2 dried bay leaves
- 2 cups water

Instructions
1. Press the Sauté button on the Instant Pot and heat the oil.
2. Sauté the garlic, jalapeno, onions, ground beef, and beef heart.
3. Continue stirring for at least 3 minutes before adding the chili powder, cumin, and oregano.
4. Season with salt and pepper to taste.
5. Add the tomatoes, bay leaves, and water.
6. Close the lid and seal the vent.
7. Press the Manual button and adjust the cooking time to 50 minutes.
8. Do natural pressure release.

Nutrition information:

Calories per serving: 439; Carbohydrates: 11.9g; Protein: 41.7g; Fat: 25.7g; Sugar: 2.4g; Sodium: 315mg; Fiber: 4.9g

Easy Balsamic Pot Roast
(Total Time: 1 Hr and 55 Min|Serves: 12)

Ingredients
- 3 pounds chuck roast, bone removed
- Salt and pepper to taste
- 3 cloves of garlic, minced
- ¼ cup balsamic vinegar
- 2 cups water
- ½ cup onion

Instructions
1. Place all ingredients in the Instant Pot.
2. Give a good stir.
3. Close the lid and seal the vent.
4. Press the Manual button and adjust the cooking time to 1 hour and 30 minutes.
5. Do natural pressure release.

Nutrition information:
Calories per serving: 217; Carbohydrates: 1.9g; Protein: 30.4g; Fat: 9.6g; Sugar: 0.9g; Sodium: 93mg; Fiber: 1.2g

Instant Pot Beef Stew

(Total Time: 1 Hr and 10 Min|Serves: 8)

Ingredients

- 2 ½ pounds beef stew meat, cut into chunks
- Salt and pepper to taste
- 4 tablespoons olive oil
- 1 onion, diced
- 2 cloves of garlic, minced
- 3 carrots, sliced
- 4 stalks celery, diced
- 1 bay leaf
- 1 teaspoon smoked paprika
- 1 teaspoon dried oregano
- 1 ½ cups water

Instructions

1. Season the meat with salt and pepper to taste.
2. Press the Sauté button on the Instant Pot and heat the oil. Sear the meat and add the onion and garlic.
3. Continue stirring for up to 3 minutes.
4. Add the rest of the ingredients and season with more salt and pepper if needed.
5. Close the lid and seal the vent.

6. Press the Meat/Stew button and adjust the cooking time to 50 minutes.
7. Do natural pressure release.

Nutrition information:
Calories per serving: 501; Carbohydrates: 22g; Protein: 43g; Fat: 27g; Sugar: 0g; Sodium: 489mg; Fiber: 14g

Italian Chicken Drumsticks with Garlic and Thyme
(Total Time: 50 Min|Serves: 4)

Ingredients
- 1 tablespoon olive oil
- 1 ½ red onions, cut into wedges
- 8 cloves of garlic, minced
- 8 chicken drumsticks
- Salt and pepper to taste
- ¼ teaspoon chili powder
- A handful of thyme sprigs
- Zest of ¼ lemon

- 1 cup chopped tomatoes
- 1 cup water

Instructions
1. Press the Sauté button on the Instant Pot.
2. Heat the oil and sauté the onion, garlic, and chicken drumstick. Season with salt and pepper to taste.
3. Cook while constantly stirring for 3 minutes.
4. Add the rest of the ingredients.
5. Close the lid and seal the vent.
6. Press the Poultry button and adjust the cooking time to 30 minutes.
7. Do quick pressure release.

Nutrition information:

Calories per serving: 486; Carbohydrates: 8.9g; Protein: 48.4g; Fat: 27.4g; Sugar: 1.5g; Sodium: 287mg; Fiber: 3.4g

WHOLE 30 DESSERT AND SNACKS RECIPES

Steamed Almond Carrot Cake
(Total Time: 40 Min|Serves: 8)

Ingredients
- 3 eggs, beaten
- 1 cup almond flour
- ½ cup Medjool dates, pitted then pureed
- 1 teaspoon baking powder
- 1 teaspoon cinnamon
- ¼ cup coconut oil
- ½ cup coconut milk
- 1 cup carrots, grated
- ½ cup walnuts, chopped

Instructions
1. Place a trivet or a steam rack in the Instant Pot. Pour a cup of water.

2. In a mixing bowl, combine all the ingredients except for the walnuts.

3. Give a good stir until well combined.

4. Pour that batter into a baking dish that will fit inside the Instant Pot.

5. Sprinkle with chopped walnuts.

6. Cover the baking dish with aluminum foil.

7. Place on the steam rack.

8. Close the lid and seal the vent.

9. Press the Steam button and adjust the cooking time to 20 minutes.

10. Do natural pressure release.

Nutrition information:
Calories per serving: 286; Carbohydrates: 6g; Protein: 8g; Fat: 25g; Sugar: 1g; Sodium: 311mg; Fiber: 2g

Thai Coconut Pandan Custard
(Total Time: 40 Min|Serves: 4)

Ingredients
- 1 cup coconut milk, freshly squeezed
- 3 eggs, beaten

- 10 Medjool dates, pitted
- 1 pandan leaf

Instructions
1. Place a trivet or steam rack in the Instant Pot and pour a cup of water.
2. Place all ingredients in a blender and pulse until smooth.
3. Pour into a strainer to collect the fibers and larger debris.
4. Pour into ramekins and cover with foil.
5. Place the ramekins on the steamer.
6. Close the lid and seal the vent.
7. Press the Steam button and adjust the cooking time to 25 minutes.
8. Do natural pressure release.

Nutrition information:
Calories per serving: 401; Carbohydrates: 49.8g; Protein: 9.9g; Fat: 21.4g; Sugar: 13.1g; Sodium: 86mg; Fiber: 25.3g

Coconut Milk Yogurt
(Total Time: 12 Hrs and 5 Min|Serves: 4)

Ingredients
- 1 coconut cream, Whole 30 compliant
- 2 capsules probiotics powder

Instructions
1. Place the coconut milk in the Instant Pot.
2. Close and seal the lid.
3. Press the Yogurt button and adjust the button so that the display says "boil".
4. Once the machine beeps, remove the lid allow the milk to cool below to 115 degrees Fahrenheit.
5. Once cool, pour the contents of the probiotics powder into the milk. Combine properly.
6. Close the lid and seal the vent again.
7. Press the yogurt button. Press the "+" button and adjust the time to 12 hours.
8. Once the Instant Pot beeps, open the lid and transfer into a sterilized mason jar.
9. Serve with your favorite fruit.

Nutrition information:

Calories per serving: 549; Carbohydrates: 11.9g; Protein: 6.5g; Fat: 62.4g; Sugar: 0g; Sodium: 7mg; Fiber: 4g

Cinnamon Bananas
(Total Time: 11 Min|Serves: 5)

Ingredients
- 12 ripe sweet plantain bananas, peeled and sliced
- 1 teaspoon cinnamon
- ¼ teaspoon nutmeg
- ½ cup water

Instructions
1. Place all ingredients in the Instant Pot.
2. Close the lid and seal the vent.
3. Press the Manual button and cook for 6 minutes.
4. Do natural pressure release

Nutrition information:

Calories per serving: 308; Carbohydrates: 56.8g; Protein: 5.5g; Fat: 7.3g; Sugar: 9.3g; Sodium: 960mg; Fiber: 17.4g

Instant Pot Almond Cake
(Total Time: 40 Min|Serves: 8)

Ingredients
- 1 cup almond flour
- ½ cup shredded coconut
- 1/3 cup Medjool dates, pureed
- 1 teaspoon baking powder
- 1 teaspoon nutmeg
- 2 eggs, beaten
- ¼ cup olive oil
- ½ cup coconut oil, freshly squeezed

Instructions
1. Place a trivet and steam rack in the Instant Pot and pour a cup of water.
2. Combine all ingredients in a mixing bowl. Mix until well combined.
3. Pour the batter into a baking dish that will fit inside the Instant Pot. Cover with foil.

4. Place on the steam rack.
5. Close the lid and seal the vent.
6. Press the Steam button and adjust the cooking time to 25 minutes.
7. Do natural pressure release.

Nutrition information:
Calories per serving: 236; Carbohydrates: 5g; Protein: 5g; Fat: 23g; Sugar: 1.2g; Sodium: 74mg; Fiber: 3g

Slow Cooker Whole30 Berry Cobbler
(Total Time: 3 Hrs and 10 Min|Serves: 6)

Ingredients
- 12 ounces raspberries, fresh
- 16 ounces blueberries, fresh
- ½ cup raisins
- ½ cup almond flour
- ¼ cup coconut milk
- ¼ cup ghee, melted
- ½ tablespoon cinnamon

Instructions

1. Place the berries and raisin in the Instant Pot.
2. In a mixing bowl, mix together the remaining ingredients until you form a dry dough.
3. Sprinkle the dough on top of the berries.
4. Close the lid.
5. Press the Slow Cook button and adjust the cooking time to 3 hours.
6. Cook on low.

Nutrition information:
Calories per serving: 202; Carbohydrates: 24.5g; Protein: 1.4g; Fat: 12.4g; Sugar: 18.3g; Sodium: 4mg; Fiber: 5.5g

Sweet Potato Puree
(Total Time: 25 Min|Serves: 6)

Ingredients
- 2 pounds white sweet potatoes
- 1 ½ cups water
- 5 Medjool dates, pitted and chopped

Instructions

1. Place all ingredients in the Instant Pot.
2. Close the lid and seal the vent.
3. Press the Manual button and adjust the cooking time to 15 minutes.
4. Do natural pressure release.
5. Transfer the contents to a food processor and pulse until smooth.

Nutrition information:
Calories per serving: 619; Carbohydrates: 97.8g; Protein: 4.8g; Fat: 24.3g; Sugar: 13.1g; Sodium: 375mg; Fiber: 14.7g

Baked Cinnamon Apples
(Total Time: 4 Hrs and 10 Min|Serves: 10)

Ingredients
- 5 peeled red apples, cored and sliced
- 1 teaspoon cinnamon
- 1 teaspoon nutmeg
- ½ cup water
- ½ cup raisins

Instructions

1. Place all the ingredients in the Instant Pot.
2. Give a good stir.
3. Close the lid.
4. Press the Slow Cook button and adjust the cooking time to 4 hours.

Nutrition information:
Calories per serving: 64; Carbohydrates: 15.3g; Protein: 0.3g; Fat: 0.4g; Sugar: 11.1g; Sodium: 1mg; Fiber: 2.6g

Sautéed Apples and Pears
(Total Time: 2 Hrs and 15 Min|Serves: 3)

Ingredients
- 1 large apple, peeled and sliced into ½ inch segments
- 1 large pear, peeled and sliced
- 2 tablespoons coconut oil
- 2 teaspoons ground cinnamon
- 3 tablespoons coconut milk, Whole30 compliant

Instructions

1. Place all ingredients in the Instant Pot.
2. Close the lid and seal the vent.
3. Press the Slow Cook button and cook for 2 hours.
4. Once the timer beeps, open the lid and press the Sauté button.
5. Allow to cook until the sauce, thickens and almost entirely evaporates.

Nutrition information:
Calories per serving: 240; Carbohydrates: 22g; Protein: 1g; Fat: 17g; Sugar: 13g; Sodium: 200mg; Fiber: 6g

Cherry Crisps
(Total Time: 3 Hrs and 15 Min|Serves: 6)

Ingredients
- 3 cups cherries
- 1 teaspoon cinnamon
- 1/3 cup coconut milk, freshly squeezed
- ¼ cup almond flour
- ¼ cup coconut flour

- 2 tablespoons coconut oil
- 1 tablespoon water
- A pinch of salt

Instructions

1. Place the cherries, cinnamon and coconut milk in the Instant Pot.
2. In a mixing bowl, mix the remaining ingredients until a lump of dough is formed.
3. Sprinkle on top of the cherries.
4. Close the lid.
5. Press the Slow Cook button and adjust the cooking time to 3 hours.

Nutrition information:

Calories per serving: 117; Carbohydrates: 12.3g; Protein: 1.3g; Fat: 7.8g; Sugar: 4.5g; Sodium: 21mg; Fiber: 5.2g

Instant Pot Applesauce
(Total Time: 5 Hrs and 5 Min|Serves: 10)

Ingredients

- 3 pounds apples, peeled and cored

- 2 tablespoons cinnamon
- 1 tablespoon nutmeg

Instructions
1. Combine all ingredients in the Instant Pot.
2. Close the lid.
3. Press the Slow Cook button and adjust the cooking time to 5 hours.

Nutrition information:
Calories per serving: 78; Carbohydrates: 20.3g; Protein: 0.4g; Fat: 0.5g; Sugar: 14.9g; Sodium: 2mg; Fiber: 4.3g

Strawberries with Coconut and Cashew Crumble
(Total Time: 3 Hrs and 15 Min|Serves: 6)

Ingredients
- 3 cups strawberries, cleaned
- ½ cup dry coconut flakes
- ½ cup cashew, ground
- 3 tablespoons coconut milk

Instructions

1. Place the strawberries in the Instant Pot.
2. In a mixing bowl, mix the remaining ingredients until a lump of dough is formed.
3. Sprinkle on top of the berries.
4. Close the lid.
5. Press the Slow Cook button and adjust the cooking time to 3 hours.

Nutrition information:

Calories per serving: 203; Carbohydrates: 16.1g; Protein: 3.5g; Fat: 15.3g; Sugar: 3.5g; Sodium: 85mg; Fiber: 6.3g

Slow-Cooked Peanut Butter Banana
(Total Time: 2 Hrs and 10 Min|Serves: 12)

Ingredients

- 4 medium-sized bananas, peeled and sliced
- ½ teaspoon cinnamon
- 2 cups almond butter, Whole30 compliant
- 5 tablespoons water
- A pinch of salt

Instructions

1. Place the banana slices in the Instant Pot.
2. Sprinkle with cinnamon.
3. Pour almond butter on top and add water.
4. Close the lid.
5. Press the Slow Cook button and adjust the cooking time to 2 hours.
6. Cook on low.
7. Once cooked, sprinkle with a tiny amount of salt on top.

Nutrition information:

Calories per serving: 206; Carbohydrates: 16.9g; Protein: 9.7g; Fat: 23.4g; Sugar: 5.4g; Sodium: 95mg; Fiber: 7.6g

Cocoa-Nut Apples

(Total Time: 3 Hrs and 5 Min|Serves: 2)

Ingredients

- 1 ½ cups coconut flakes
- 2 tablespoons 100% cacao powder, unsweetened

- 1 tablespoon cacao nibs, raw
- 1 ½ teaspoons cinnamon
- 1/8 teaspoon nutmeg
- 1 red apple, peeled and sliced

Instructions
1. Place all ingredients in the Instant Pot.
2. Close the lid.
3. Press the Slow Cook button and cook for 3 hours.

Nutrition information:
Calories per serving: 371; Carbohydrates: 52.7g; Protein: 3.4g; Fat: 18.4g; Sugar: 34.6g; Sodium: 184mg; Fiber: 11.4g

Natural Fruit Preserves
(Total Time: 6 Hrs and 5 Min|Serves: 12)

Ingredients
- 1 cup fresh blueberries
- 1 cup fresh raspberries
- 1 cup fresh blackberries

- 1 ½ cup dried pineapple, sugar-free and air-dried

Instructions
1. Combine all ingredients in the Instant Pot.
2. Close the lid.
3. Press the Slow Cook button and adjust the cooking time to 6 hours.

Nutrition information:
Calories per serving: 21; Carbohydrates: 5.1g; Protein: 0.5g; Fat: 0g; Sugar: 2g; Sodium: 0mg; Fiber: 0.9g

CONCLUSION

The Whole30 diet is all about eating the right kinds of food devoid of any artificial flavors and preservatives. Thus, you are basically eating healthy and delicious meals to revert your system by taking advantage of clean eating. With this particular diet, you will be able to address different health issues such as diabetes, high blood pressure, and obesity. Since you only eat food made from whole food ingredients, you also clean your palate so that you can enjoy more natural foods.

Eating healthy does not mean that you have to content yourself from eating tasteless and boring foods. In fact, there are so many delicious that you can whip up following the Whole30 protocol thus you have no excuse not to eat healthy while munching your favorite comfort food. And while preparing meals using whole food ingredients can take a lot of time, using the Instant Pot saves the day as you can prepare healthy and delicious meals with just a touch of the button and half the time you normally would on stovetop cooking.

I hope that you can try all the recipes in this book and be amazed that you don't have to sacrifice taste and quality to bring your health back.

www.ingramcontent.com/pod-product-compliance
Lightning Source LLC
Chambersburg PA
CBHW071907070526
44583CB00016B/1885